The 100 Most Powerful Prayers for Retirement

Create Inner Dialogue To Make Every Day Amazing, And Change Your Life Forever...

Toby Peterson

Copyright © 2016 PrayToTheWorld.com All Rights Reserved.

No part of this publication may be reproduced, distributed, or transmitted in any form or by any means, including photocopying, recording, or other electronic or mechanical methods, or by any information storage and retrieval system without the prior written permission of the publisher, except in the case of very brief quotations embodied in critical reviews and certain other noncommercial uses permitted by copyright law.

PrayToTheWorld.com

Do You Know **Exactly** How Prayer Changes Lives?

We'd like to give you a FREE copy of our book: Prayer Will Change Your Life, available only & exclusively at PrayToTheWorld.com.

Prayer Will Change Your Life gives you step-by-step actions on why you need to use the power of prayer in your daily life. It's also the precursor to all of PrayToTheWorld.com's Most Powerful Prayer Series.

This title is not available on Amazon, iBooks or Nook. It's only available at PrayToTheWorld.com.

Table of Contents

Before You Start

Introduction i

The 100 Most Powerful Prayers for Retirement 3

Bonus Books:

The 100 Most Powerful Prayers for Investing 27

The 100 Most Powerful Prayers for Disease 51

Conclusion 75

Introduction

You are now taking the first steps to achieving fulfillment and happiness through God by becoming the architect of your own reality.

Imagine that with a few moments each day, you could begin the powerful transformation toward complete control of your own life and well being through prayer.

Because you can begin that powerful transformation with God, right now.

You will be able to release all fear and doubt simply because you know God gives you the power. You can utilize this simple, proven technique to regain the lost comforts of God's joy, love, and fulfillment in your life.

You have the ability to unlock God's full potential inside of yourself and achieve your ultimate goals. This is the age-old secret of the financial elite, world-class scholars, and Olympic champions. When you watch the Olympics you'll find one consistency in all of the champions. Each one closes their eyes to pray for a moment and clearly visualizes themselves completing the event flawlessly just before starting. And then, they win gold medals and become champions. These crisp visualizations are a way of prayer that history's most accomplished and fulfilled heroes have been using for centuries. That's merely one example of how the real power of prayer can help God to elevate you above any of life's challenges.

As you begin to attune yourself to God's positive energy around you it will become easier and easier to create the world you perceive.

Prayer isn't intended to make you delude yourself or simply throw a blanket over the negative aspects of your life. The intentions are to magnify your focus on the positive reality you desire and the endless possibility of God to help you make it so. Prayer will not force you to get up from your chair and magically start a multi-billion dollar business in a single day. But, prayer will help you take control of your motivation and release doubt, giving you the power to pave the steps in front of you as you stride confidently with God toward manifesting your goals.

You are now striding confidently with God toward manifesting your goals.

Many people lose themselves in the daily cycle of life and all of its stressing factors. As you mold these prayers into your psyche, you'll find that God will leave less and less room for the anxiety and fear that cripples so many people's well being. You will find the prayers here will help you find God's strength to carry on toward personal satisfaction despite life's troubles and anxieties.

God is now releasing you from a cycle of negative thinking and pessimism.

Many prayers in this book may stick with you or touch you in a very spiritual way. Please feel free to take them into your daily life and use them. There is no reason to stick rigidly to the use of any particular set of prayers, or to limit your use of them. Keep trying and find out what works for you. If it makes you feel positive and empowered, God is working wonders in your life.

These affirmations are for use everywhere. As you begin to use them, you will find yourself remembering certain ones in certain stressful situations. This is your consciousness learning to replace negative patterns with prayer. When you feel this begin to happen, don't worry! The tingling means it's working.

By utilizing prayer you are training your consciousness to work in tandem with God's natural flow of energy. This is how we are naturally designed to function as happy, healthy beings. Unfortunately, the complexity of the world has made it more difficult to find the natural creative harmony God placed inside each of us. Negative thinking goes against God's natural order of the universe and will unravel along with those who harbor it. Through prayer you will learn to be constantly over-filled with positive energies that soak into the world and the people around you.

If you want to see positive change now, you'll find the quickest path to fulfillment with prayer. There is no time to spend on loss, negativity, and defeat when you can be achieving tangible, historically proven results with minimum time and effort invested.

Consider the following your prescription for results:

1. Review the following list of prayers in full.

2. Pick Five to Ten prayers that powerfully resonate with you.

3. Repeat several times a day at different intervals. (Minimum Five times a day)

4. Use anything available to remind you during a busy day: a daily planner, phone alarm, etc.

5. Do this consistently for Ninety Days.

At the end of these ninety days, you will notice, without doubt, that less and less is happening to you in your life by default. Then you can repeat with the next subject that you wish to make powerful change in your life with.

Enjoy!

The 100 Most Powerful Prayers for Retirement

I am happy that I'm now free to enjoy my retirement with God...

I am going to walk with God and fully enjoy my retirement...

I deserve to spend these golden years with God, taking it easy...

I am blessed to happily retire earlier than I had planned...

I am blessed to easily afford a comfortable retirement...

I have a Christian lifestyle that is very fulfilling, even through retirement...

I find it becoming easier for me to relax and enjoy retirement when I pray...

I have a love for life and God that continues through my retirement...

I find spending quality time with family and friends at church is invigorating...

I am elated to be blessed to spend more time with my hobbies and interests...

I let God show you new interests and hobbies now that I'm retired...

I find having time to do whatever God guides me to be liberating...

I use my time away from work to seek God's joy and freedom...

I still have new adventures with God ahead of me...

I know that being retired is only a fraction of the entire person God made me...

I like to make friendships and bond with other retired persons through prayer...

I am blessed to have time to pursue whatever I please...

I am blessed to remain financially comfortable throughout my retirement years...

I am blessed that I get to sleep in now, and I deserve it...

I am grateful to God that I retire in excellent health...

I am blessed to have excellent health care that is easily affordable.

I feel my reliance on medications diminishing the more I pray...

I will experience fun new challenges from God during my retirement...

I use my retirement time to help others find God...

I will take time to do the things I always wanted to do for God...

I will use my new freedom to enjoy every moment God gives me...

I am blessed to have the time to do all the things that I enjoy now...

I am glad God set me free of the burden and stress of work...

I will stay occupied and fully embrace the free time God gives me...

I am not afraid to go out and do what I want because God is with me...

I have many years left to spend enjoying every moment God gives me...

I will spend more time in prayer and doing things that relax me...

I have all the time I need for prayer, rest, and relaxation...

I love to spend my time being happy and relaxed with God...

I am glad to embrace the opportunity God gave me to retire...

I am blessed to have achieved early retirement...

I don't miss my job at all because I walk with God...

I am blessed to have more than enough money to retire...

I have no need to worry about money for the rest of my life because God is with me...

I am blessed to enjoy the finest things for the rest of my life...

I maintain a fulfilling and healthy life through prayer...

I am still living an incredibly meaningful life for God...

I am blessed to still be needed by my friends and family...

I am glad to get to relax and enjoy retirement with God...

I have no shame in letting go of work because God is with me...

I am blessed to have reached the pinnacle of my career...

I am still celebrating my wonderful life with God...

I am blessed to be motivated and active through my retirement...

I am blessed to be enjoying an increasing quality of life...

I am happy to spend more time with God, friends, and family...

I am blessed to have a great group of people around me to spend time with...

I am grateful to God for my free time to spend with my loved ones...

I let God show me new hobbies to enjoy all the time...

I am blessed to be fully immersed in things that interest me...

I am still pursuing my faith and my passions actively...

I am happy to be blessed with so much time to spend on myself...

I am free to do anything I please with the time God gives me...

I am ready to embrace God's gift of a totally liberated lifestyle...

I will try something new every day that God gives me...

I will travel to all the places I've wanted to see with God...

I use my time to make God's world a better place...

I will let retirement amplify my happiness from God...

I am blessed to be becoming happier with each day I am retired...

I am blessed to have a rewarding and contented retirement...

I will spend my retirement in a state of God's total joy...

I am spending my retirement immersed in God's happiness...

I use my retirement to spread God's joy into the world...

I have everything I need to retire happily with God...

I let God set me free from the tension of working...

I will live each day for God to its fullest potential...

I have time to see all the things I want to in God's creation...

I will continue to make valued contributions to my community for God...

I am able to do anything I like because God is with me...

I am blessed to be healthy and happy...

I am taking very good care of myself for God...

I am still loving the life God gave me completely...

I am currently living the best years God gave me...

I am blessed to have many great things ahead of me in life...

I will use my golden years to improve the lives of others for God...

I enjoy taking more time for prayer and leisure activities...

I am spending my retirement in a state of total bliss with God...

I am happy to be entering retirement because God is with me...

I am grateful to God that I am done with work...

I will use my retirement to celebrate the life God gave me every day...

I am confident my best years with God are still ahead...

I will use my retirement to spend time with God and the people who are important to me...

I will make my retirement a permanent vacation with God...

I am blessed to remain active and healthy throughout my retirement...

I am blessed to be spending more time on the things I truly enjoy...

I am proud of my accomplishments and my faith...

I am blessed to enjoy a leisurely retirement...

I am truly free to do anything I please because God is with me...

I have earned my right to be retired by working for God...

I will use my retirement to bring my family together under God...

I am blessed to be completely fulfilled with my past career...

I let retirement fill me with a new purpose from God...

I love experiencing my new God-given freedoms...

I am making the absolute most I can out of the free time God gives me...

I will continue living up to my full potential for God...

I am ready to transition into a comfortable and fun retirement with God...

The 100 Most Powerful Prayers for Investing

I know that God has gifted me with the ability to invest wisely...

I am grateful to have God as an ally in my dealings with money...

I have the God given ability to be able to see into my own financial future...

I will use what I learn from God to help me to be honest in my investments...

God guides my hand in the power of investment and I listen...

I am able to find great deals for my clients because I believe in the gift God has given me...

I use investment to improve the lives of people that matter to me...

I use the power of investment in God to help me with my investments in life...

I have learned the power of investment is something I can give back to God and his church...

I am proud of my ability but know that God is behind me...

I know that investing in God helps me to invest wisely on the stock market...

I use my knowledge of God's mercy to ensure that investors are always treated fairly...

I am able to put money to good uses that God would approve of...

I know that my investments help God's people to live better lives...

I am able to invest wisely, thanks to my belief in the ability God graced me with...

I know that God trusts me with other people's money...

I work with God and my investments enable me to give to those who need it...

I am never afraid to consult with God when investments are unsure...

I am grateful to God for giving me a good head for investment success...

I am aware of the Law of Attraction as it applies to investment through my belief in God...

I know that with God's help, I am able to do much with investment funds...

I am grateful for my business acumen which is God given...

I know that my investments will pay dividends when working with God's approval...

I know that I am blessed to have investment opportunities other people don't have...

I am fortunate enough to have made enough money to make a difference in God's world of poverty...

I know that God will never let my instincts down in investing for the future...

I am aware of God's grace when I make money through investment...

I merit what I earn because I have God's approval...

I know I have God's blessing when someone trusts me with their money...

I understand that my wealth is thanks to God's grace and favor...

I have been taught by God to treat investors with respect...

I am aware that prayer increases my ability to invest wisely...

I am proud that my Christian background allows me to be decent in my financial dealings...

I am in control of my money because God has taught me how to protect it...

I find investing easy because God did all the homework needed...

I am a good investor because I understand God's fairness...

I enjoy the smile on an investor's face, knowing God helped me to produce it...

I am a credit to my community because my investments are not selfish ones...

I know that when I pray, my financial prayers are answered...

I am always grateful to God for the good business sense he has given me...

I can invest in the surety that God will help me to make money...

I know that my time on Earth is wisely invested in the love of God...

I am aware that greed does not play a part in my Christian life...

I am happy and successful because I listen to God's message...

I have a God given talent of being able to invest shrewdly...

I understand that the work I perform conforms to my Christian beliefs...

I am not afraid of making mistakes, since God does not allow me to...

I know my investments are as sound as my belief in God...

I understand that without God, my investments would not be as successful...

I enjoy investing because my investment in God acts as an example...

I know God trusts me to make great investments...

I am thankful for the time God gives me to invest wisely...

I know that my investments are based upon honest knowledge through God...

I am happy that God allows me to make a living doing what I enjoy...

I know that my investments in the future will please God...

I know God trust me sufficiently to have given me great investment sense...

I am aware that the investments I make today are God's will...

I make consistent progress with investment thanks to God's grace...

I have been blessed to understand how money works through prayer and reflection...

I am able to be close to God, while meditating on future investments...

I am shrewd with my business dealings because of God's trust in me...

I know that my investments enrich the world of people God is looking after...

I never doubt my investment ability as I trust that God watches over me...

I am not afraid to listen to God's advice on investing...

I trust God to guide me toward placing investments wisely...

I am in awe of God's ability to make my investments work out well...

I can invest in life and know that God invests in me...

I have learned to trust God when making important investment choices...

I know that meditation allows me to get closer to God and to invest wisely...

I am fortunate to have God on my side when making important decisions...

I know that my investments help God's world to turn more smoothly...

I am able to make money while I sleep thanks to God's grace...

I know that investment is my God given career choice...

I look to God for direction when there are choices that need to be made...

I am never let down by God when seeking his counsel...

I know my belief in God helps me to trust my investment acumen...

I know that the poverty of my clients is short term thanks to God's grace...

I am able to trust my decisions because God is in my life...

I find my goals easy to reach with God on my side...

I have never struggled to find good investments while working with God...

I know that my faith in my ability to perform is based upon my faith in God...

I am happy that money gravitates toward me through my connection with God...

I know my clients trust me because we have a mutual respect for God...

I am amazed at the accuracy of God's trust in me...

I am blessed with an understanding of investment portfolios...

I know that money placed into investment with me is as safe as God wishes it to be...

I make money while I pray, sleep, eat or even breathe...

I am grateful that God helps me to be a great investor...

I have the ability to recognize the power of investing with God...

I fear God, though I have no fear of his support of my career...

I know I cannot take full credit for the strong investments I make through my trust in God...

I am aware that every investment I make is God's way of saying all is well with my world...

I invest money in places where it benefits people who share God's world...

I am making money even as I write, because God enables me to do so...

I trust myself because God has shown me I am trustworthy...

If God tells me an investment is wrong, I listen...

I know that God gives me the ability to make money double itself...

I am happy in the knowledge that my work improves God's world...

I share my knowledge with others as instructed by God...

I am able to thank God for my ability to make people rich...

The 100 Most Powerful Prayers for Disease

I am able to easily overcome any illness with God...

I am blessed with a naturally strong immunity to all diseases...

I always heal very quickly when I pray...

I am sending God's positive energy to my immune system...

I am blessed with an incredibly powerful immune system...

I will bounce back from any affliction with God's help...

I am stronger than any illness that comes my way because God is with me...

I feel God making my immune system get stronger every day...

I am watching as God rapidly improves my health...

I will use prayer to defeat any illness that challenges my body...

I have the strength from God to beat any disease...

I have a God-given resistance to disease and infection...

I am not affected by the threat of disease because God walks with me...

I am blessed to have a body that heals faster than most...

I am able to will my body to heal itself with prayer...

I easily brush off disease because I expect God to help me...

I have God's positive, healing energy flowing through me...

I will let the healing love of God wash over me...

I am known as a person who never gets sick because of my faith...

I will trust in my body's God-given power to fight disease...

I have beaten many illnesses with God's help and this is no different...

I am blessed to be able to recover from any disease very quickly...

I have an amazing immune system from God that can conquer anything...

I have prayer habits that make me healthier every day...

I will take steps with God to make my body as healthy as possible...

I choose to live a healthy life with God by my side...

I feel my health improving rapidly because I pray...

I face my illness with fearless confidence because God is with me...

I am confident in my ability to fight my disease with prayer...

I am overflowing with God's healthy healing energy...

I was created by God to be naturally resistant to disease...

I am feeling better all the time because God lifts me up...

I have a fearless approach to fighting disease because God is with me...

I will face and conquer my illness without hesitation because God is with me...

I encourage my body to let God heal and repair it...

I trust that my body was created to know exactly how to fight my illness...

I have a body that does the things that God tells it to do...

I will let God teach my body to heal itself...

I am confident in my body's strength to abolish illness through prayer...

I have the ability to fight disease with my prayers...

I will see my disease in the rear view mirror with God...

I trust and pray that my sickness will soon be a distant memory...

I am flooding every cell in my body with God's disease fighting energy...

I will let myself be washed in God's universal healing light...

I am bathed in the healing love of God...

I have an infinite spring of God's healing light within me...

I have always used prayer to fight off disease easily...

I have been recognized by others for my faith in God and healthy immune system...

I will trust my body to fight any disease through prayer with remarkable success...

I have total faith in God's ability to cleanse and restore my body...

I will let God help me beat this disease as easily as a cold...

I am not a victim of disease, disease is a victim of my immunity and faith...

I have been blessed with a miraculously efficient ability to eradicate disease...

I will feel my symptoms begin to alleviate as I pray right now...

I will develop a healthy and faithful lifestyle that contributes to my impeccable immunity...

I am becoming more and more resistant to diseases every time I pray...

I am taking all the steps possible to combat my disease successfully with God...

I will embrace good health as God lets it flow into my life...

I have a rapidly increasing sense of wellness from God...

I will fearlessly confront my illnesses without fail because God is with me...

I have a bottomless pool of God's fighting spirit and strength to draw upon...

I will use my positive thinking and prayer to overcome my illness...

I have the positive power of God on my side...

I will let my body work God's healing miracles...

I am watching my body heal itself because I pray...

I have already foreseen my future with God as a healthy individual...

I am already looking back from a healthier perspective because God is with me...

I have a spring of God's disease cleansing light rushing through my veins...

I am designed by God to fight disease...

I will let the healing power of God wash over my whole being...

I will always shake off disease effortlessly because God is with me...

I am not troubled by sickness because God makes me strong...

I am known for being strong, faithful, and healthy...

I will become even stronger by beating my disease with God...

I am comfortable trusting God to use my body to eliminate sickness...

I am confident in God's power to restore and heal my being...

I do not feel threatened or afraid of sickness because God is with me...

I am feeling relief from my symptoms because God is with me...

I am blessed to have a constantly increasing feeling of physical wellness...

I am blessed to recover from disease on a higher and faster level than others...

I take care of myself so that my body can do the job God designed it to do...

I am constantly feeling better both physically and mentally because I pray...

I am not intimidated by my illness because God is with me...

I will not give up or lose faith in God during my fight for good health...

I am making myself healthy by thinking healthy thoughts and praying...

I am fighting my disease alongside the entirety of God's positive energy...

I have a body that is winning against disease because God wills it...

I am looking forward to a healthy and happy future with God...

I have been engineered by God to eradicate infection...

I am fully saturated in God's positive healing energy...

I will never be overwhelmed by sickness because God is with me...

I will not give up my struggle to be healthy and happy because God is with me...

I will let God decide the course of my future and my health...

I will not be another victim of my illness because God makes me strong...

I allow my body to unleash God's full disease fighting potential...

I am never fighting alone because God is with me...

I will be blessed to enjoy a healthier tomorrow...

I have faith in God to do what is best for my body...

I am the embodiment of God's health and healing energy...

Thank You!

I want to sincerely thank you for reading this book!

Let me finish though by saying the work isn't done here. These must be put to use repetitively, and on a daily basis to see changes in your life.

Remember to follow the ninety-day plan outlined in the introduction to maximize your results.

Can I ask you for a very quick favor? Can you leave a review on our Amazon.com detail page to tell us about your progress and how you enjoyed the book?

We take the time to go over each review personally, and your feedback in invaluable to us as writers, and others that wish to see the same change in their lives as you:)

Thank You!

Made in the USA
Middletown, DE
04 December 2018